Meet The Numbers

Poems Inspired by Numbers

David Horner & Mike Jackson

About Us

Mike Jackson and David Horner are Goodeyedeers.

David is the author of the 26 short poems in this book. After the poems, he explains their different poetic forms and gives some fascinating facts about some of the numbers we use every day

There is also a section at the end of the book outlining how Mike used AI (Artificial Intelligence) when creating the images for this book.

Meet the Numbers - Introduction

This collection of short poems is meant as a companion to **The 26**, a book in which each letter of the English alphabet has a chance to speak for itself and tell something of its story.

Meet the Numbers lets numbers do the same thing. There are many more numbers than letters, of course, and so this is very much a random selection, featuring just 26 of the numbers between – and including – zero to one million.

Each poem is in a fresh poetic form – different to the ones featured in **The 26** – taken from different cultures and times. There are details and descriptions of the forms after the poems.

Finally, there are a few, hopefully, fascinating facts about the single digits 0 to 9: where they came from; how they got their modern names and shapes; some of the places they have featured in works of art, literature and music.

David Horner

I'm odd. I'm prime. I'm lonely.
So, good to see you, my dears.
There's not much I can tell you,
till February appears.
Then, oh, I feel quite giddy –
will this be one of those years?
Or, disappointed once more,
odd and prime and bored to tears.

Me? A crowd, wise monkeys,
score and ten, blind mice, bags
full, D, Rs, bears, cornered,
shepherds, musketeers. Cheers.

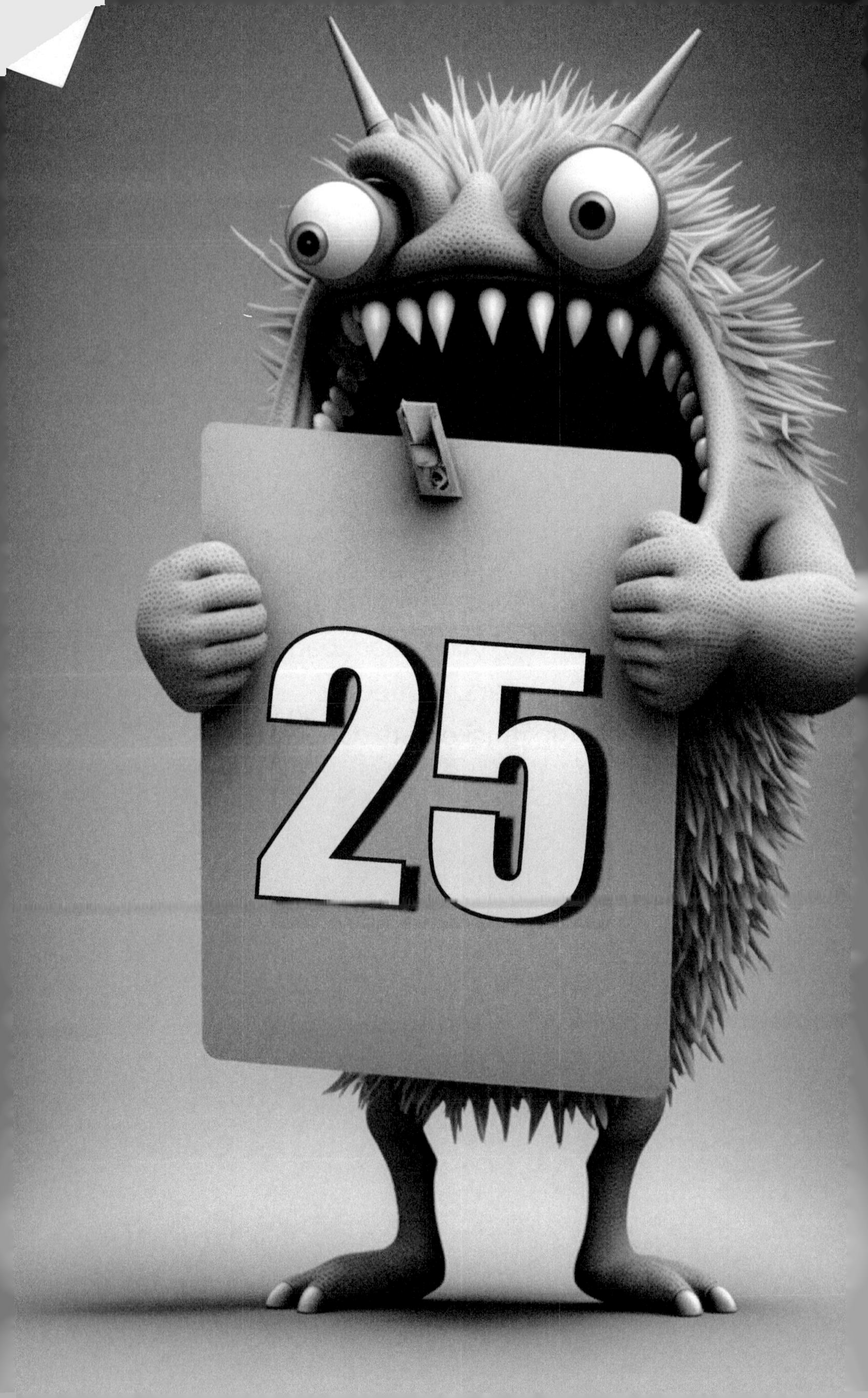
25

Although I'm what you call a square,
I'm also all the years you'll sleep.
That's every shuteye, snooze and kip,
in nursery, bedroom, open air;

with every dream and each nightmare,
the snoring, once you've counted sheep,
for though I'm what you call a square,
I'm also all the years you'll sleep.

And yes, I've clocked that brief affair –
but mum's the word, so not a peep.
For secrets are the things I keep.
Let's say they're just for us to share,
as though I'm what you call a square,
I'm also all the years you'll sleep.

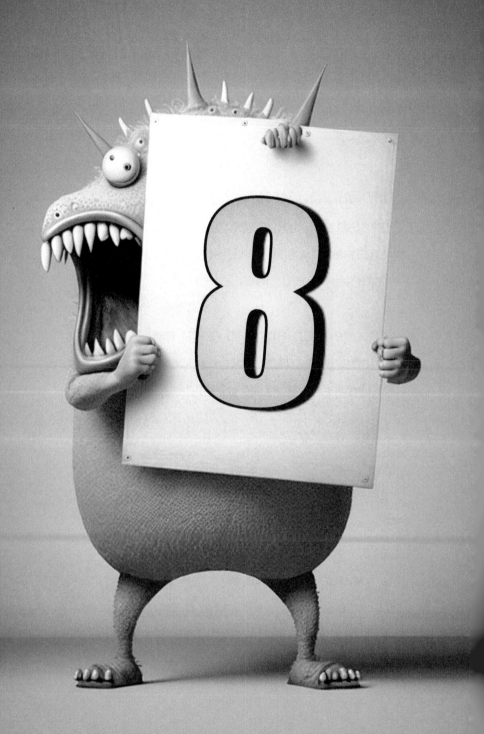

Take four from me and leave just the same.
Take a quarter, leave half a dozen.
Take three quarters and leave a couple.
Take half of me and leave nothing.

Whenever pens or pencils stroll around a white page,
or we're summoned to appear on some screen,
we look out, we numbers, blinking at the sudden light
and quietly think over what might have been.

Our purpose is answering your several purposes,
but in our servitude, we take small delight
in dreaming of different, three-dimensional lives:
one of us an hourglass, one a bird in flight;

one would be a balloon on a string, one a seahorse,
a mast and yacht's sail, a wheel for the potter,
a ship's prow, a candle, a stalk and ripe cherry.
And me? A white swan, tall on ink-black water.

Between zero
and ninety-nine,
reader, you'll find,
remarkably

I'm the daddy -
syllabic'ly
at least. Clearly
my USP.

It could have been so very different.
All Babylon once counted on me.
But now another rules the world.
I should be glad to have disappeared.

All Babylon once counted on me.
Yes I, 60, was their foundation.
Schoolroom sums, traders' deals, me, all me.

But now another rules the world.
Your 10s, your 100s, your – I understand, though
leaving me with just these scraps?

I should be glad to have disappeared,
like Lighthouse and Gardens, and not
be here, counting seconds, counting minutes.

The way
heart can make earth,
thing make night, palm make lamp,
and astronomers moon starers;
and just
as canoe makes ocean, so I,
eleven plus two, make
exactly twelve
plus one.

Of course, I know that Michael Jordan,
Shane Warne, David Beckham, have chosen

me. And I hear, Alessia Russo.
I'm flattered. However, I want you

and I to visit Rome, the Senate,
where, expected any minute,

this March day, Julius Caesar - warned:
The Ides have come but not yet gone.

Aloft, aloof, the feared dictator.
Up step Cassius, Cimber, Casca,

and more. See each small knife strike
through shoulder, cheek, thigh, chest and neck.

So very many blows rain down
this early springtime afternoon

in Rome in 44 BCE.
How many in all? The answer's me.

The one I feel sorry for's 43.
Because, in the matter of muscles, he
is how many you need to frown. Dearie me.
So much just to show your disgruntlement.

How extravagant, how wasteful, while
I am the few you use to make your smile.
And in my ordinariness, yes, I'll
admit: it is my Mona Lisa moment.

I've a puzzle I'd like you to see:
write down the numbers 1 to 9
and add just three arithmetic symbols to find
a sum that makes – me!

Come some Friday mornings I sense your apprehension.
Just certain Friday mornings, your growing apprehension.
And I accept it's all my fault – though never my intention.

I'm aware I'll never number any hotel floor.
12 goes straight to 14 when you want a hotel floor.
And no one, no one wants me stuck on their front door.

Now some of you blame Judas, say that he's the cause.
Thirteenth at that supper, he's got to be the cause.
Then that Apollo moon-shot – never won me no applause.

You choose your own sweet reasons, hell I aint no sleuth.
I'd love to know your whys of it, but no, I aint no sleuth.
But aint I the unlucky one? Aint that the blessed truth?

Guilty? Certainly, but surely
only by association?
Neither of us meant to murder
in our special operation.

Hello to you, dear reader. The name's 15.
And I've a small sum for you – please have a go.
Just add my two digits, then those in between.
Answer? Yes, 15! I add up to me. So,
now, because you're clever, can you discover
the next, the one, the only other number
where the sum of the sequence of each digit
makes itself? One clue: reach 30, you've missed it.

My name, my letters, my worth: four. And unique. Coincidence, you say. I say an honour.

When life begins? Could not care less.
That time spent in the wilderness?
It's flattering but no, forget
all that and let me now confess

my self-love lies in how I'm spelt –
like *ghost, almost, begins, abet.*
One single simple quality:
we're ordered as the alphabet.

To me no triviality
and something more than rarity;
among us numbers, uniqueness.
I know. I know. Such vanity.

Three digits, me. Your safeness is my need.

       For my cream tea, this service suits my need.

Emergent seal, what fresh fish do you need?

       Sweet marjoram - *this* is the herb you need!

Field marshal, say which sergeant you now need.

       The C of E – which surplice do you need?

Etude in C: a cellist's what you need.

       Imagine sea – where surf is all you need.

O merchant, seize what servants you do need.

       Your majesty, which hairpiece meets your need?

Misfortune? Hey, rich heiresses you need.

       Hermione, the soothsayer is your need.

The Martians say what surfaces they need.

       Emergency, which service do you need?

Not day's building blocks, nor the king's *tasty dish,* but rather those boots that disturbed the moon's sleeping.

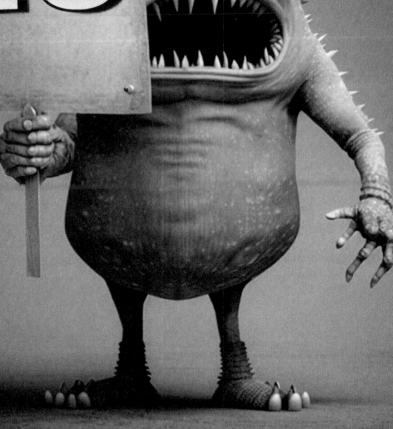

One among so very many: 46,
that's me. However, I do hold a small charm,
a secret, one which, if you care to learn, take
up your Bible and turn its pages to Psalm
46. Count to its forty-sixth word: *shake.*
Remember this and go on to the psalm's end.
Now, carefully count back and make no mistake,
the forty-sixth word, I promise you you'll find
is *spear.* Thus, with no kidology, no tricks,
I've shown to you the mystery that I guard,
that buried deep within me lies the Bard.

Sextilis mensis, that was me. Sixth month

across that empire without end.
Until ten months became twelve

and my days renamed for
Caesar Augustus, reducing me
to mere *sex,* and schoolboys' sniggering.

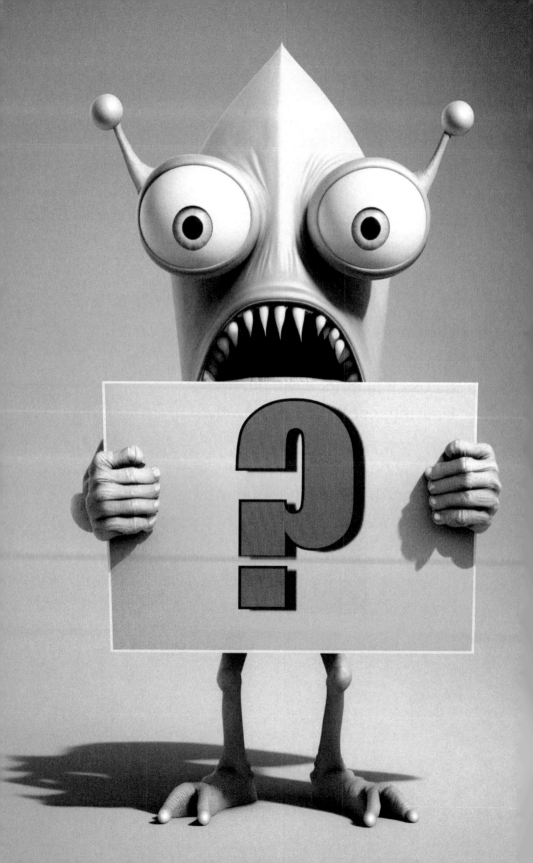

My first is in paws but isn't in feet.

My second's not in parrot but is (twice) in parakeet.

My third's not in guitar but is in violin.

My fourth is in hero and also heroine.

My fifth is in beans but nowhere in cucumbers.

My whole, you seem to think, is the luckiest of numbers.

So, let's get one thing perfectly straight –
no ifs, no buts, no maybes.
Though some among us love your little *jeu de
mots,* I'll not be two fat ladies.

I'm not about to lend my name to such childish
pantomime. Dirty knees and clickety-clicks;
rhyme and pun and – and what, I ask, is trombone
time? Quite frankly it's

humiliating. But as you find such follies
fascinating, and wanting this to stay a polite
tête-à-tête, in future know me as two swallows
gyrating through high summer's light.

I'm zero, null, nada, nowt, nix.
So many words to name me nothing.
What's worse is, I might not exist.

Those Greeks and Romans would insist
that nothing could not then be something.
I'm zero, null, nada, nowt, nix.

The plain truth is I'd been dismissed
and who could bear such snubbing?
What's worse is, I might not exist.

And if I'm gone, will I be missed?
It's so unkind, so unbecoming.
I'm zero, null, nada, nowt, nix.

It's hard to stay an optimist;
my self-esteem's past crumbling.
What's worse is, I might not exist.

I fear there'll be no sudden fix.
Not odd, not even, not anything,
I'm zero, null, nada, nowt, nix.
What's worse is, I might not exist.

We all love it, of course.
Fahrenheit 451,
1984,
The 39 Steps, Catch –
me. Until it was not.

Imposter syndrome.
Isn't that what you call it?
I'm grateful, of course,
for all you've made of me.
The best of the best.
But just take a look at me:
stick-thin, soldier-straight;
and then those that come after,
their strokes, their swirls, their
curlicues. You see, don't you?
One is one and all alone –

In the USA
the record books say
that he

begins one June day
to count out loud *chez
lui.*

Live-streamed for fair play
he makes his way
to me.

The 26 Poetic Forms

29
Lüshi

Mine is inevitably only a pale imitation of this Chinese form. Chinese uses characters not letters for its writing, so it's impossible to imitate the form fully. A lüshi is a traditional form written in classical Chinese. Usually, a lüshi is eight lines long, with five, six or seven characters in each line. I've had to make do with seven syllables per line, but I have kept the lüshi's convention of having the same rhyme on each even-numbered line.

3
Gzha

This is a Tibetan folk form. There should be just four lines, each of six syllables. Gzhas need no rhyme, but they should always finish with two stressed syllables to give the poem a definite conclusion.

25
Rondel

This is one of those forms imported from the French troubadours. These poets and composers flourished from the 11th to the 13th centuries. Geoffrey Chaucer was writing his rondels in the mid 14th century. Other examples of the troubadour tradition are the villanelle, used elsewhere in this book, and the triolet and rondelet which you can find in **The 26**. French rondels repeat the opening two lines at the poem's end, to serve as a framing device. English poets added a repetition of those two lines in the middle, and I've kept with that tradition. Those repeated lines establish the two rhymes used exclusively throughout the form, making an ABba abAB abbaAB sequence.

8
Brhati

This is a very old Vedic – or early Sanskrit form - dating from around 1500 to 500 BCE. There can be any number of verses, but each one should be made of 36 syllables, set down in four lines with nine syllables per line.

2
Doha

Another Indian form, this time from the Hindi and also Urdu tradition. A doha is written in very long 24 syllable lines, with a break (or caesura) in the middle to make two lines of 13 and 11 syllables. The two-line couplet can usefully be set out as a four-line quatrain with the rhymes coming at the ends of lines 2 and 4. There is no set number of lines to a doha and it is a form often used for longer narrative poems.

77
Pathya Vat

A very trim form from Cambodia. A pathya vat can be just four short lines long with lines 2 and 3 rhyming. When new stanzas are added, the last line of the previous stanza sets the rhyme for lines 2 and 3 in the following one. So, for **77**, the rhyme scheme is abbc dcce.

60
Trimeric

The American Walter A. Stone came up with this form. I can find no biographical details for the gentleman, so sometime in the last century is the best I can do for a date of the form's invention. A trimeric has four stanzas. The first has four lines, and the following three stanzas have three lines each. The clever touch is that those three stanzas begin by repeating the respective line of stanza 1. So, stanza 2 begins with stanza 1, line 2; stanza 3 with stanza 1, line 3 and stanza 4 with stanza 1, line 4.

11
Butterfly Cinquain

Born in New York in 1878, the unforgettably named Adelaide Crapsey invented the cinquain. It's a five-line form, in a 2, 4, 6, 8, 2 syllabic sequence. There is an example in **The 26.** Adelaide died aged only 36 and so couldn't know the huge popularity, not only of her basic idea, but also the variants it spawned. The butterfly cinquain is just one of those. It's a nine-line poem, starting with the original cinquain pattern and then reversing it with 2, 8, 6, 4, 2 syllable lines to create the butterfly shape on the page.

11's poem is all about anagrams and here are a few more good ones: schoolmaster / the classroom; the Morse Code / here come dots; listen / silent; the countryside / no city dust here; William Shakespeare / I am a weakish speller.

23
Knittelvers

A German form, sometimes called Knüttelvers, which translates as 'cudgel verse'. It first appeared in the Middle Ages and was popular until the 17th century when it came to be seen as mere doggerel. Some even tried to have the form banned, claiming it was of no artistic value. Revived a century later as a genuine German form, today it tends to be used for parody, satire, even children's poems. Knittelvers are built with pairs of rhyming lines – couplets – each line having 8 or 9 syllables. A basic rhythm is created by having four stressed syllables to each line.

17
Ochtfochlach

This is one of the simpler Irish forms. An ochtfochlach has eight lines, rhymed aaab cccb. No other rules at all, it seems.

100

Dribble

A dribble has just one rule: it must have exactly 100 letters. And to be clear, spaces, punctuation marks, symbols are not included in the count. The name derives from the mini-fiction form, the drabble, a story written in 100 words. Drabbles were invented in the 1980s by the Birmingham University Science Fiction Society. They took the term from Monty Python's Big Red Book of 1971, in which a word game, Drabble, appears. Players have to write a novel and the first to finish is declared the winner. The SF Society came up with the 100-word rule. A later Drabble Project published an anthology of 100 drabbles, with copies costing 100 shillings. All proceeds went to charity.

Back to the dribble, and the answer to 100's puzzle is $123 - 45 - 67 + 89$.

13

Blues

Very definitely African American in origin, the blues as poetry emerged in the 20th century out of the earlier song tradition. It is sometimes called Blues Stanza. It takes the basic song form of three lines to every stanza, rhymed aaa bbb, etc. In each stanza, line 1 makes a statement; in the sung blues, line 2 usually repeats line 1, but in blues stanzas, this line rephrases or develops line 1. Line 3 then acts as a response to those opening lines. For really great blues stanzas, look no further than the poems of Langston Hughes (1901 – 1967).

19
Chatushka

A four-line form from Russia. The name in Russian means to speak fast. A chatuska to Russians is rather like the limerick to us, being used for satire and comedy. When chatuskas are performed live, there is usually some musical accompaniment. There are chatuska competitions in Russia, in which contestants must compose their poems on the spur of the moment There is no fixed rhyme scheme but in each 8-syllable line, the stresses should fall on the odd syllables. So: **Gui**lty? **Cert**ainly, but **sure**ly, / **on**ly **by** ass**oc**iation.

15
Strambotto

This is an early Italian form, dating from the 12th Century. In the 16th Century strambotti were often set to music. There are three varying forms of the strambotto, but all three specify a stanza, or multiple stanzas, of eight lines. Each line requires eleven syllables and is thus called hendecasyllabic. Each of the three variants has its own rhyme scheme:

> the Strambotto Siciliano has abababab
> the Strambotto Toscano has abababcc
> the Strambotto Romagnuolo has ababccdd.

There is a theory that this 8-line form is a forerunner of the 14-line sonnet.

The answer to 15's 'small sum' is as follows: 1 + 2 + 3 + 4 + 5 = 15 and the only other sequence that works in the same way is: 2 + 3 + 4 + 5 + 6 + 7 to give the answer 27.

4
Landay

This Afghan form comprises just two usually unrhymed lines; the first has 9 syllables and the second, 13. So, 22 in all. The only other convention is that the landay should end with the sound 'na' or 'ma'. Landays are part of an oral tradition going back thousands of years, created by and for illiterate people. However, today they have become a means for Pashtun women to express themselves and their defiance of male oppression, sometimes sung aloud to a drumbeat, or written down and sometimes appearing in public as graffiti. The word 'landa' in Pashto can mean a short and deadly snake.

There is a wholly fascinating article on the landay past and present online at www.poetryfoundation.org/media/landays.html

40
Rubaiyat

Rubai is a Persian term for a quatrain. A rubaiyat is the anglicised version of the Arabic word for a collection or sequence of rubais. The form was popularised in English by Edward Fitzgerald, who in 1859 published his translation of 'The Rubaiyat of Omar Khayyam'. Robert Frost's poem 'Stopping by Woods on a Snowy Evening' is a twentieth century example, showing how long the form's popularity lasted. What links the stanzas of a rubaiyat together to make an Interlocking Rubaiyat is the rhyme scheme; stanza 1 is rhymed aaba; stanza two makes its rhyme from that unrhymed line in verse 1 to become bbcb. In the final stanza, the third line picks up once again the main rhyme of stanza 1 and so in 40's poem ccac.

999
à la Bartholomew Griffin

Sadly, the only thing we know for certain about Bartholomew Griffin is that he was buried on December 12th, 1602. The rest is a matter of 'perhaps' and 'probably'. Perhaps he read to Queen Elizabeth as part of the entertainment when she visited Kenilworth Castle in 1572; he was probably from Coventry and a lawyer. He was certainly a gentleman, and like most Elizabethan gentlemen, he wrote sonnets. He is credited with inventing a variant of the sonnet form – hence its description, translating as 'in the style of Bartholomew Griffin'. Perhaps he got bored with just composing sonnets, or he found the demands of the rhyme scheme wearying. Whatever the reason, in his variant, he simply used the same word at the end of each line.

By chance, the question that is the origin of 999's tomfoolery is an exact line of iambic pentameter, those sonneteers preferred rhythmic pattern:

Emergen**cy**, which **ser**vice **do** you **need**?

24
Kimo

This is the Israeli version of the Japanese haiku. So, 10, 7, 6 syllables in three lines, rather than the haiku's familiar 5, 7, 5. Kimos usually require a focus on stillness, with images held like snapshots.

46
Onzijn

This is a recent invention from Holland. It is basically all about the number 11. An onzijn has 11 lines, each with 11 syllables. The rhyme scheme is abcbcdcdaee. The onjin (also known as an elftel) was devised in 1983 by a Dutchman known as drs. P – his real name was Heinz Hermann Polzer. He was a writer, cabaret performer, academic, composer, and, like Tom Lehrer, he accompanied his own songs on the piano. He used his onjins to introduce his guests on his arts magazine programme Babel.

6

Cherita

One line, then two lines, then three lines: a cherita. Cherita is the Malay word for story and so a Cherita should tell a story. The form was created as recently as 1997 by ai li, a UK based poet and artist of Malay heritage. Ai li has a whole website devoted to his creation, www.thecherita.com.

7
Charade

This bit of fun began life in France in the 1700s, where it was very much like our party game charades today. In the mid 18th Century, it reached England where it became a written word game, popularised in magazines of the day.

It is also known as a riddle-me-ree. Not exactly a poem, it is nevertheless a puzzle in a literary form. The answer to the puzzle is always a single word spelled out letter by letter in the clues hidden in each line. The concluding line is often a final clue to the whole word.

88
Lento

A contemporary American form created by Lencio Dominic Rodrigues and named by its inventor – about whom nothing else appears to be known. In many ways it's just a conventional four-line form, with the even lines rhymed. What makes the form a bit different is the requirement that the first words of each stanza's four lines should also rhyme. The form allows for 2-, 4- and 6-verse lentos, but unfortunately 88, in wanting to be just a bit different, insisted on 3.

0
Villanelle

As the name suggests, this is French form, though probably Sicilian in origin. Its form became fixed early in the 17th Century and has lasted to this day. Dylan Thomas's 'Do Not Go Gentle into that Good Night' is one especially good example. A villanelle is a highly structured form composed of five three-line stanzas plus a final four-line stanza. Lines 1 and 3 of the first verse reappear alternately in the following stanzas and return together as the closing lines of the whole poem. A villanelle has only two rhymes, so, using capital letters for the repeated lines and lower case for the rhymes, the rhyme scheme is:

A1bA2 abA1 abA2 abA1 abA2 abA1A2

18

Flamenca

This is a short Spanish form of just five lines in a 6, 6, 5, 6, 6 syllable sequence. One nice rule is that lines 2 and 5 shouldn't rhyme but use assonance instead. Assonance uses either matching vowel sounds as in 'cake' and 'late', or matching consonant sounds as in 'clock' and 'chick'. The flamenca is also known as a seguidilla gitana, or gypsy folk song.

It is true that Joseph Heller originally called his novel Catch-18. He was asked to change it when it was learned that Leon Uris's publisher was about to launch his novel called Mila 18 and Heller's publishers feared the confusion and resulting loss of sales.

1

Choka

This term in Japanese means 'long poem'. And true to its name, a choka can be any length the poet fancies – so long as it is an odd number of lines altogether. Chokas began life in the Japanese royal court as early as the 6th century and lasted until the 14th. Basically, a simple form, alternating 5- and 7-syllable lines and concluding with two 7-syllable lines to give the required odd number total.

1,000,000

Bergerette

This is a French song form dating from the 16th century. A bergerette is nine lines long in a 5, 5, 2, 5, 5, 2, 5, 5, 2 syllable sequence. It takes its name from 'bergère', French for shepherdess. The six longer lines rhyme and the three short lines have a second rhyme. Two or more bergerette stanzas for a single poem is called a virelai.

In 2007, between June 18th and September 14th, Jeremy Harper, a computer engineer in Birmingham Alabama, spent 16 hours of 89 days counting out loud to one million. He stayed at home throughout and never shaved, live streaming the whole endeavour. He raised over $10,000 for charity and his achievement is registered in the Guinness Book of World Records.

Notes on the Numbers

0

As 0 says in the poem, it's a digit with a problem: the Ancient Greeks had no symbol for zero. They were very uncertain about it, even hostile to using it - how could nothing be something?

In Ancient China, they represented zero with just a 'vacant position'.

The term zero comes originally from the Arabic word 'sifr', meaning empty.

Things got better for it in India, where 0 began life as a large dot, eventually appearing as an O symbol in the manuscripts of a third century handbook of arithmetic for merchants and traders.

Even today, 0 is different – it's neither an odd nor an even number and it's neither positive nor negative. However, taking on its egg-shape has given zero a particular status: the French *l'oeuf* has morphed into love in tennis and a duck's egg, shortened to duck in cricket, both indicate a score of nothing.

Some Starring Roles

Much Ado About Nothing - William Shakespeare 1598
Love Minus Zero/No Limit - Bob Dylan 1965
Symphony No. 0 - Anton Bruckner 1869
Zero for Conduct – Jean Vigo 1933
Less than Zero - Brett Easton Ellis 1985
Hawaii 5–0 - CBS tv 2010

Back to the ancient Greeks, and once again they didn't consider 1 to be a number at all. They did acknowledge its existence – *oinos* was their term for the single dot on dice – but as multiplying and dividing by it got you nowhere, they saw no use for it. They also treated it as both odd and even, arguing that when you added it to an odd number it made an even one and adding it to an even number made an odd one.

The importance of 1 today is visible in the language. There is a clear link between the English words one and 'a/an'; words like 'union', 'unique' and 'universal' come straight from the Latin word for one, *unus*; there is a close relationship between 'one' in English and *un* in French, *ein* in German, *en* in Danish, etc.

'One' has a range of grammatical functions: a pronoun, as in *One needs regular exercise;* a noun, as in *one plus one;* a determiner as in *one step at a time.*

A key feature of 1 is that it has retained its shape right from its origins in India around 3 BCE, where, as today it was a simple vertical line. Adding a serif or curved stroke to the top can cause unnecessary confusion with 7.

Some Starring Roles

Another One Bites the Dust – Queen 1980
The No. 1 Ladies' Detective Agency – Alexander McCall Smith 1998
Capricorn One - Peter Hyams 1978
One Day in the Life of Ivan Denisovich – Aleksander Solzhenitsyn 1962
One Foot in the Grave – BBC tv 1990
No. 1 (Royal Red and Blue) – Mark Rothko 1954

The ancient Geeks, yes them again, found 2 a weird number, simply because of this:

$$2 + 2 = 2 \times 2.$$

Surely multiplication should do more than addition? Well, not in this unique case, no.

Even today, as 2 is the smallest prime number – divisible only by itself and 1 – despite being the first even number, it is sometimes called 'the oddest prime'.

Two's name comes from the Old English words *twa* and *tu.* Its middle 'w', still heard in the German *zwei,* returns to audibility in words such as 'twin' and 'twice'.

The number 2 began life in ancient India around 3 BCE as two short horizontal lines, much like our contemporary equals sign. Modern Japanese and Chinese script use this form to this day. In Arabic writing, the lines twisted round, then formed first a symbol rather like the letter 'p', before becoming our modern digit, with its bottom line echoing that Indian original.

Some Starring Roles

A Tale of Two Cities – Charles Dickens 1859
Daisy Bell (Bicycle Built for Two) – Harry Dacre 1892
The Lord of the Rings: The Two Towers - JRR Tolkien 1954
The Two Gentlemen of Verona – William Shakespeare 1594
One Fish, Two Fish, Red Fish, Blue Fish – Dr Seuss 1960
Two Up, Two Down – BBC tv 1979

At last, those ancient Greeks are happy: they have in 3 their first real number. Why real? First, because, unlike 1 and 2, 3 has a beginning a middle and an end; second 3 x 3 makes more than 3 + 3 unlike that odd number 2. The Greeks also held that 3 was the first male number, with all subsequent odd numbers being male and all even numbers female.

The use of three lines to denote the number three has been very common: horizontal to this day in Chinese writing; vertical in BCE Indian and Roman script. Somewhere around 1 CE, in Sanskrit writing, those lines got rotated to the horizontal, later with the top two lines given a small downward stroke on the right.

Cursive writing connected the strokes and added short curves to the top and middle strokes plus another at the now open end of the bottom stroke to give the shape we have now. Today, interestingly a curved or flat top to the number is quite acceptable.

Some Starring Roles

Three Men in a Boat – Jerome K Jerome 1889
Three Times a Lady – Lionel Richie 1978
Richard III – William Shakespeare 1593
Three Men and a Baby – Leonard Nimoy 1987
The Three Musketeers – Alexandre Dumas 1844
Three Sisters – Anton Chekhov 1900

In ancient India, 1, 2 and 3 were written by just using the required number of lines to represent each number. 4 got its four lines but joined together to make a cross, just like today's plus sign. Extra details were added over time until Arab traders simplified it once again, and to make the writing of it quicker, joined the left arm to the top vertical. This meant the number could be written in one stroke in a shape closely resembling today's 4. In pre-!2th century Old English, the word 'feower' can be found.

Some ancient Greeks, especially the followers of Pythagoras, called any number divisible by 4 'even-even', linking it to matters of harmony in the world. There were the four elements, making up the universe: earth, fire, air and water; four humours: blood, yellow bile, black bile and phlegm, each impacting a person's well-being and needing therefore to be kept in balance. Hence, for example, the idea that bleeding could re-balance and restore someone's health.

The importance of 4 can be seen today in such things as the four Gospels, the four seasons, the four corners of the earth, even Franklin Roosevelt's Four Freedoms. And we still go on hunting the elusive four-leafed clover in the hope it will bring us good luck.

In !852, Francis Guthrie, an Englishman, asked himself the question, 'How many different colours would be needed to colour a map of the world so that no two adjacent countries have the same colour?' He decided he'd need just four colours; however, his answer has been often challenged and to this day, no wholly accepted answer has been achieved.

Some Starring Roles

Four Women – Nina Simone 1989
The Sign of the Four – Arthur Conan Doyle 1890
The Four Seasons – Antonio Vivaldi 1720
The Four Horsemen of the Apocalypse – John the Revelator 1 CE
The 4.50 from Paddington – Agatha Christie 1957
Four Quartets – T S Eliot 1943

The first strange thing about 5 is that unlike 1, 2, 3 and 4, it doesn't appear anywhere in early Indian numeracy. The second strange thing is that when it does show up in Arabic scripts, its shape bears no relation to how it looks today. It begins like a capital Y, then as an upside-down h, later a lying down y, a backward facing 3, then back to the upside-down h before European mathematicians came up with today's 5.

Obviously, today's digit bears no relation to the Roman V. It is thought that this came about because when counting to five on the fingers of a hand, a V is made by the space between the open thumb and first finger. The Romans didn't add I before or after V to make 4 or 6 in their writing. This habit emerged in 14th Century Europe with the development of printing, only to disappear as Arabic numerals replaced the Roman ones

Old English had the word 'fif' and modern Dutch has 'vijf'.

The Greeks, particularly disciples of Pythagoras, linked the number five to marriage. This is because 5 is what you get when you add 2, their first even, female number to 3, their first odd, male number.

The Hindu god Shiva is sometimes shown with five faces. These relate to his five divine activities: creation, preservation, destruction, revelation and delusion. At a less exalted level, Pluto has five moons, Enid Blyton had her Famous Five, and Wilbert Awdry's James the Red Engine bears the number 5.

Some Starring Roles

Take Five – Paul Desmond 1959
Five Children and It – E Nesbit 1902
Five Easy Pieces – Bob Rafelson 1970
Symphony No. 5 – Ludwig van Beethoven !804-8
Five Ways to Kill a Man – Edwin Brock 1990
Slaughterhouse 5 – Kurt Vonnegut 1969

The evolution of this digit is a lot more straightforward than 5's. As early as 250 BCE it shows up as a Brahmi (Indian) numeral, in pretty much the same form as it has today, though initially rather like a turned round 'e'.

The Ancient Greek word for six was 'hexa' and this survives as a prefix in 'hexagon', for example. The Latin term 'sex' we again use as a prefix as in 'sextet', 'sextuplets', 'sexagenarian'. Anyone born with six fingers on one hand or toes on one foot is said to be sexdactyly.

The Pythagoreans were even keener on 6 than 5. They linked the latter to marriage- see Note above - and 6, they believed was connected to both marriage and health. This is because 6 is what you get when you multiply 2 (their first even, female number) by 3 (their first odd male number). 6 also represented balance as in two triangles shown base on base.

St Augustine (354-430 CE) was so fond of this digit, he wrote, 'Six is a number perfect in itself … God created all things in six days because this number is perfect. And it would remain perfect, even if the work of six days did not exist'.

Some Starring Roles

The Inn of the Sixth Happiness – Alan Burgess 1957
Six-Dinner Sid – Inga Moore 1991
The Six Wives of Henry VIII – Naomi Capon and John Glenister, BBC tv 1970
Six Handbags - Andy Warhol 1958
Six Characters in Search of an Author – Luigi Pirandello 1921
Now We Are Six – A A Milne 1927

At the start, Indians wrote 7 like an upside-down capital J, with a curved top to the stroke. Arab writers flattened the top stroke over time and made the downward stroke a diagonal - as we do today.

A prime number is any whole number that can only be divided by 1 and itself. So, to begin, 2, 3, 5 - and 7. Of all of them in the 1-10 sequence, 7 is known as the 'most prime' – because that's all it is. The numbers 1, 2, 3, 4 and 5 can be doubled and still stay within the sequence; 6, 8 and 10 can be divided in half and leave whole numbers; 9 is divisible by 3. 7, however is 7 and nothing more. It's arithmetically unique.

Yet 7 crops up everywhere: the days of the week, the seas and continents of the earth, the wonders of the ancient world, notes in a scale, the deadly sins, the dots on opposing sides of dice, the black spots on most UK ladybirds, the hills on which Rome was built.

People in the Middle Ages believed the rainbow had five colours. When Isaac Newton split light using a prism, he saw those five colours - and added two more (orange and indigo) to make seven, so convinced was he of the importance and necessity of the number.

If a boy is the seventh son of a seventh son, then he's not just considered lucky but possessed of magical powers.

Some Starring Roles

The Magnificent Seven – John Sturges 1960
Seven Little Girls (Sitting in the Back Seat) – Paul Evans 1996
Seven Brides for Seven Brothers – Stanley Donen 1954
The Seven Last Words of Our Saviour on the Cross – Joseph Haydn 1787
White Iris No. 7 – Georgia O'Keefe
The Seven Year Itch – Billy Wilder 1955

8 is a lucky number for many Chinese as their word for eight sounds very like their word for 'prosperity'. The word eight is clearly the trickiest digit to spell correctly; and once learners have mastered it, they have the related problems of how to spell 'eighteen' and 'eighth'. Logic might suggest 'eightteen' and 'eightth' but logic isn't always how English spelling works.

The word eight clearly derives from the early German 'ahto', and the Latin 'octo'. The latter survives as a prefix in, for example, octopus, octet, octuplets. In Old English there's 'eihta', which may be where those spelling problems began.

Today's digit 8 derives from Arabic numerals, though its first appearance, as so often in early Indian scripts had it shaped like the sign for bends in the road, twisting first left, then right. Later, it looked like a quickly scrawled 5, then with added flourishes, it resembled a capital S until finally, the flourishes were joined up to make the modern double loop.

The symbol for infinity, which first appeared in the 17th Century, is often described as a lying down or sideways figure eight, though the two are quite unrelated. The term 'pieces of eight', found in so many stories of piracy on the high seas, comes from 16th Century Spain, where a Spanish dollar was worth 8 reales.

Some Starring Roles

Eight Cousins – Louisa May Alcott 1875
Eight Days a Week – John Lennon and Paul McCartney 1964
I'm Henery the Eighth, I Am – Fred Murray and R P Weston 1910
Number 8 – Jackson Pollock 1949
When Eight Bells Toll – Alistair McLean 1966
Eight Tales of Terror – Edgar Allan Poe 1846

Sometime in the 3rd Century BCE, Indians wrote 9 very much like our '?' but without the dot. Next it morphed into something like a 3 and after that the bottom curve was curled right round the whole digit like today's '@', though in a clockwise direction. Arab writers modified it again, extending the curl straight down. With the '3' reduced to a simple circle, it took on pretty much the shape we have today. In Old English we find 'nigon' and 'nyne' and in even earlier Sanskrit texts 'nava'.

Nine is thought by some in China to be a lucky number because it sounds like their word meaning long-lasting. Nine is also closely linked to the Chinese dragon, a traditional symbol of power. However, the Japanese hold the opposite view as their word for nine sounds like the Japanese word for suffering.

Up to 2006, Pluto was accepted as the ninth planet in order from the sun after Mercury, Venus, Earth, Mars, Jupiter, Saturn, Uranus and Neptune. Suddenly Pluto was relegated to the status of dwarf planet. A shame as the change also rendered obsolete the excellent mnemonic 'My Very Easy Method Just Speeds Up Naming Planets'.

In Spain it's held that cats have seven lives; in Turkey only six and in the English-speaking world it's nine. The origins are unknown but there is an old rhyme that seemingly details the years and stages of a cat's life: 'A cat has nine lives. For three he plays, for three he strays and for the last three he stays.'

Some Starring Roles

District 9 – Neil Blomkamp 2009
The Nine Tailors – Dorothy L Sayers 1934
Zero through Nine – Jasper Johns 1961
Inside No. 9 – Reece Shearsmith and Steve Pemberton, BBC tv 2014
The Makers of Rome: Nine Lives – Plutarch 120
9 to 5 – Dolly Parton 1980

The 26 and AI

AI (Artificial Intelligence) has recently become a talking point with many people. As AI continues to develop, it is likely to play an even more significant role in our lives, transforming the way we work, live, and interact with the world around us.

In this poetry book we have used AI to generate our colourful monsters holding the numbers. The software we used is called Midjourney. This allows text prompts to be used as a starting point or inspiration for creating generative art. The process involves using machine learning algorithms to analyse the text and generate visual representations of the text.

For this book we simply put in the text prompt - *'wacky monster, crazy style, holding a blank sign'* and Midjourney gave us a series of unique and crazy monsters.. I then added in the numbers. (AI is still not good with numbers and text!)

We hope you love them as much as we do!

AI is only going to get more incredible in terms of what it can generate. We plan to take full advantage of all that it can offer. There are exciting times ahead of us.

Mike Jackson

Meet The Numbers - Talking Book

We thought it would be fun to create a free talking book version of 'Meet The Numbers'.

Use your smartphone or tablet to scan the QR code below and you will be taken to a version of this book where you can sit back and listen to David reading each of the 26 poems.

We hope you enjoy it.

David & Mike

Goodeyedeers

THANK YOU

For buying this poetry book

We do hope you have enjoyed reading the poems in this book.

All the money raised from the sale of this book goes to a children's charity MedEquip4Kids.

Based in Manchester, MedEquip4Kids improves the health of babies and children in the UK by providing hospitals with equipment not available from limited NHS resources.

Since 1985 MedEquip4Kids has raised over £24 million to fund neonatal and paediatric medical equipment, sensory and play facilities in hospitals, specialised equipment for disabled children and mental health support.

Scan this QR code to find out more.....

Check out the Goodeyedeers blog to see what else we get up to and have a look at some of the other books and educational resources we create.

Goodeyedeers

Printed in Great Britain
by Amazon